I Miss You, Brother

Written by Judy Drake
Illustrated by Lekshmi Bose

I Miss You, Brother

JUDY DRAKE

Copyright © 2021 by Judy Drake

All rights reserved. No part of this publication may be reproduced, distributed, or transmitted in any form or by any means, including photocopying, recording, or other electronic or mechanical methods, without the prior written permission of the publisher, except in the case of brief quotations embodied in critical reviews and certain other noncommercial uses permitted by copyright law. For permission requests, write to the publisher, addressed "Attention: Permissions Coordinator," at the address below.

Judy Drake/Author's Tranquility Press
2706 Station Club Drive SW
Marietta, GA/30060
www.authorstranquilitypress.com

Publisher's Note: This is a work of fiction. Names, characters, places, and incidents are a product of the author's imagination. Locales and public names are sometimes used for atmospheric purposes. Any resemblance to actual people, living or dead, or to businesses, companies, events, institutions, or locales is completely coincidental.

Ordering Information:
Quantity sales. Special discounts are available on quantity purchases by corporations, associations, and others. For details, contact the "Special Sales Department" at the address above.

I Miss You, Brother/ Judy Drake. -- 1st ed.
Paperback: ISBN: 978-1-956480-62-7
E-book: ISBN: 978-1-956480-63-4

In loving memory of my son Frankie. I love you so much and miss you terribly.

Thank you, Kevin, for allowing your thoughts to be part of this story. Thank you, Chad and Shawn, for bearing with me.

I miss you, brother! Sometimes I think you will be home very soon, but you don't come home. I wish you could. Mom and Dad are so sad. I am afraid to leave them. I want you to come back so they won't be sad anymore.

I miss playing with you. I know you do too! Is it OK that I talk to you? I already do, but I'm not sure if I am supposed to. Are you OK at your new home? I wonder if you miss me like I miss you.

I would like to talk to Mom and Dad about you, but they sometimes cry a lot when they hear your name. Am I not supposed to talk about you? I don't want to be bad and make them cry. If I upset them, that would be bad. What if I say something and they think I am just being silly? I am not trying to be silly at all!

Sometimes Mom and Dad are afraid to let me go outside and play. Sometimes they want me to stay in the same room with them. I do not understand what I did wrong. Am I being punished? Is it my fault you are not here? The grownups are always whispering when they talk. Sometimes when they have friends over, I can play in another room.

I want to tell you I was in sitting on your bed when your friends came to visit. They looked surprised and I did not think they wanted me there. I left quickly because I did not want them to be mad. I just wanted to be with you. I guess they just wanted to be with you too.

Sometimes brothers share the same room and sometimes they each have their own room. Is it OK if I sleep in your bed? I think I will feel safe in your bed. I promise I will not touch any of your things. This will always be our room from now on.

Am I allowed to wear your favorite hat? Maybe someday, can I please borrow your favorite T-shirts and your jacket?

Remember how we played with cars and blocks? Can I pretend you are still playing with me? Sometimes I like to be alone though. Is that alright? Sometimes I just want to look at our toys. Do I have to share our toys when Mom and Dad's friends bring their boys and girls to visit Mom and Dad? Why don't my friends just come to visit me?

I love to remember how funny you were. You made me laugh. You made funny faces, told me jokes, and sang silly songs. There are so many other things you said and did that always made me laugh. I have some great memories.

Sometimes I think about you and worry about you. Did it hurt when you went away? Do you hurt now? Can you see me? Can you hear me?

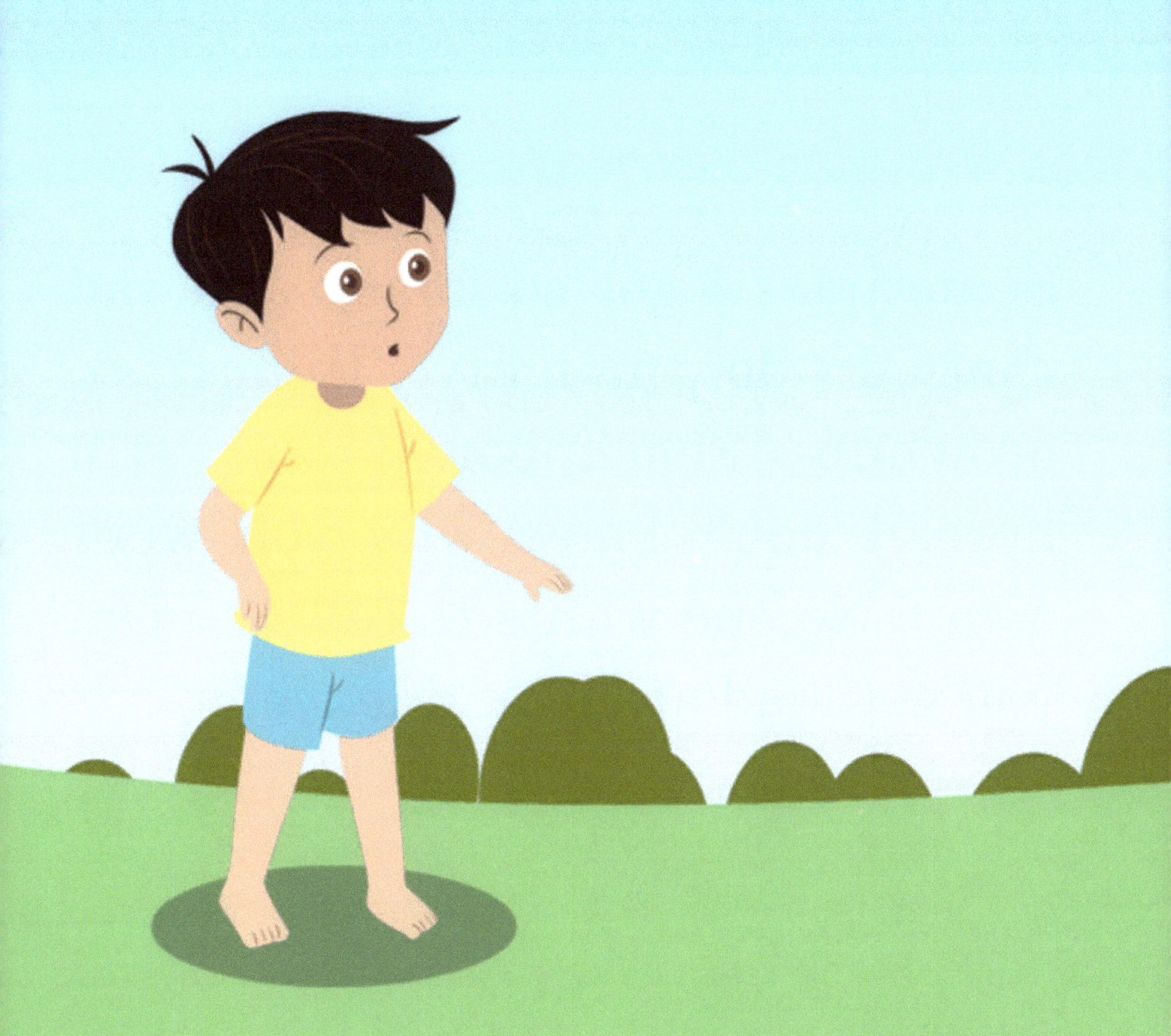

Sometimes I get so lonely and sad that I do naughty things so grownups remember I am still here. I don't know why you went away. No one wants to tell me. Did you get mad at me and leave?

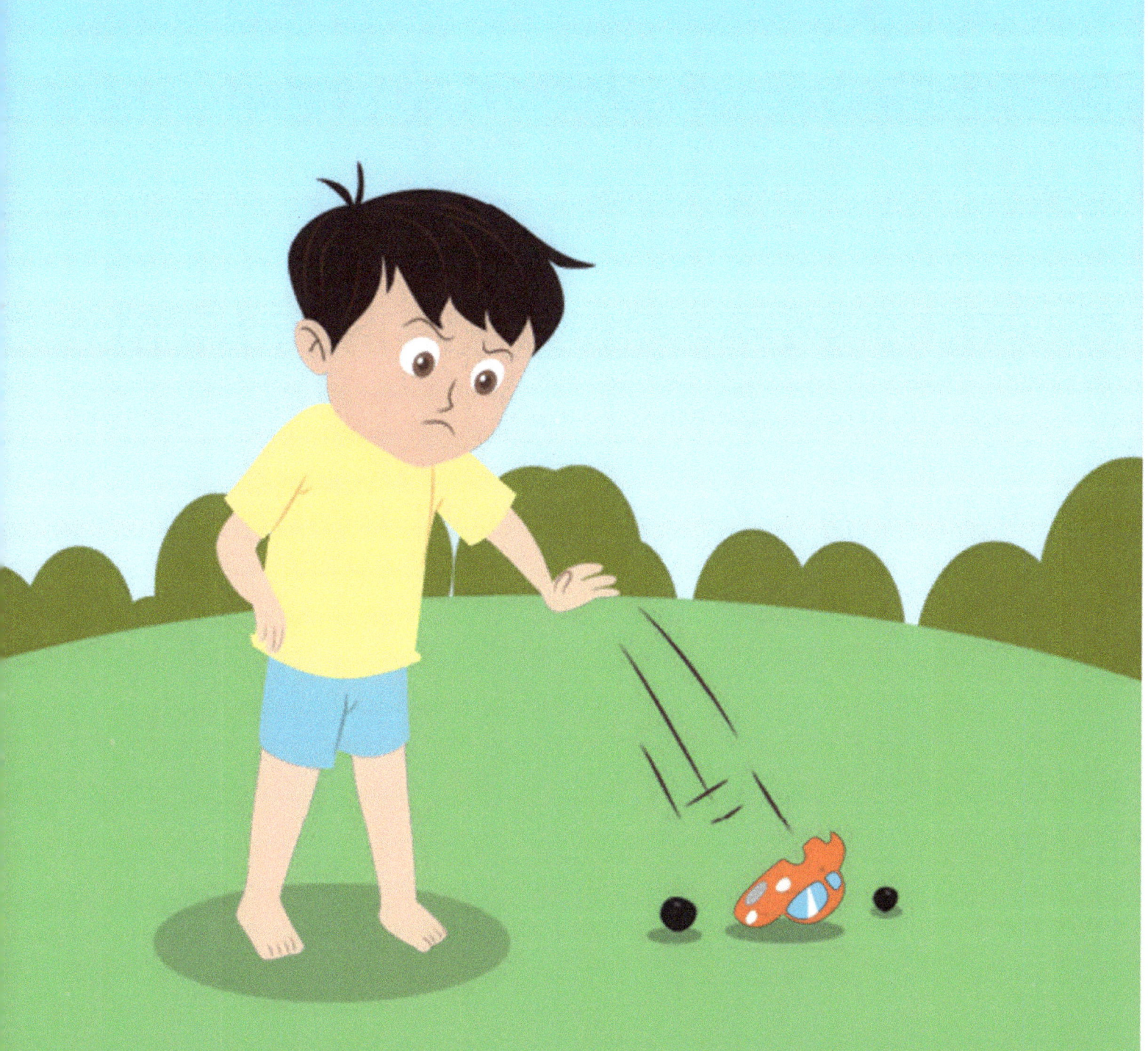

Will I leave Mom and Dad just like you did? Will I be the same age? Will I know when my last day will be here? Can I say good-bye or do I just leave?

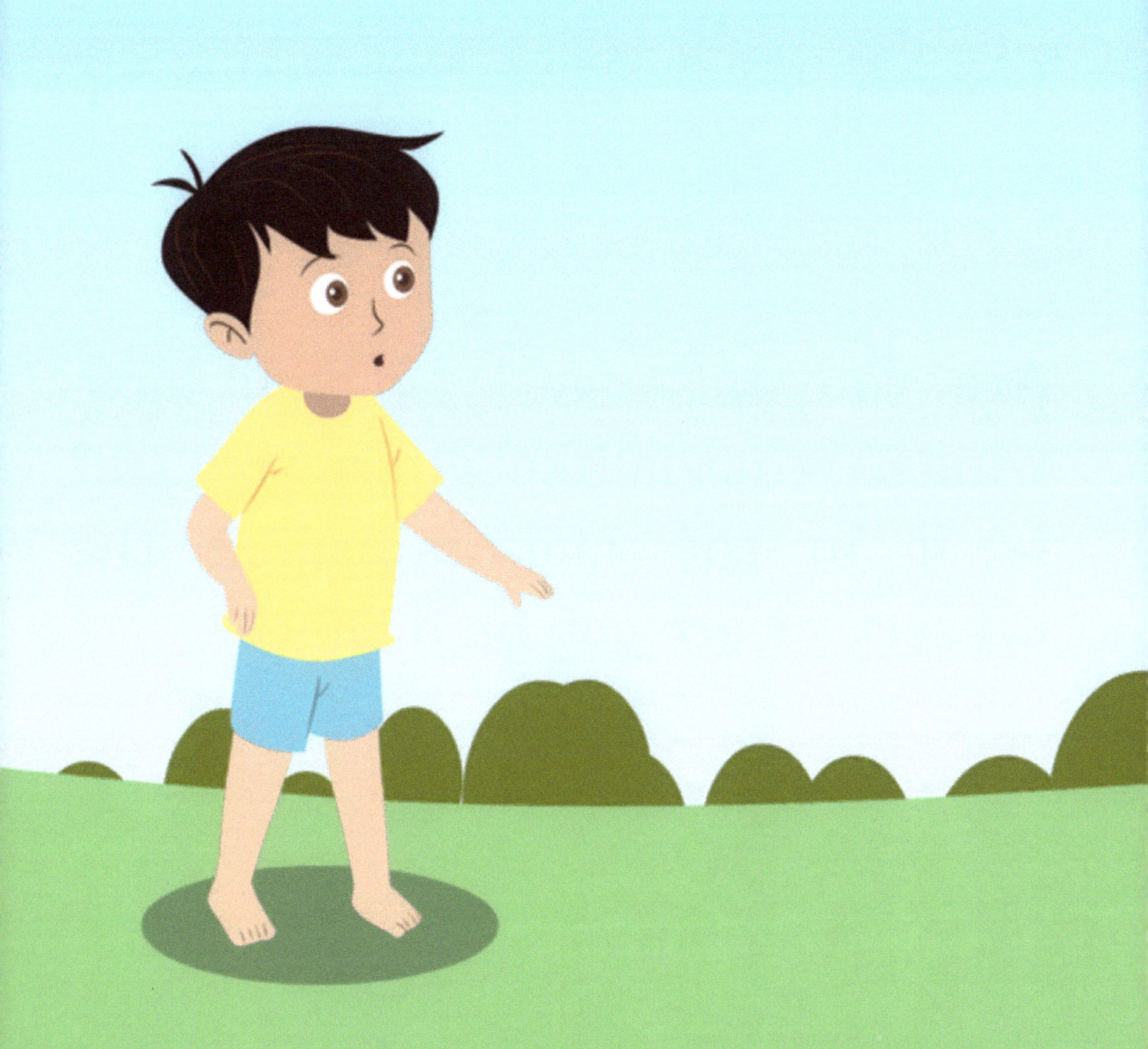

Are you an angel? Do you have wings? What is like where you are? Is it in the mountains, or the dessert, or are you on a beach?

Maybe tomorrow I can draw a picture of us and put it in a balloon to send to Heaven for you to keep. I hope that makes everyone smile again. I will know when you get it because I won't be able to see the balloon anymore.

I miss you, brother. I am afraid I might stop remembering you, but I really don't think that will happen. I love you and think about you every day.

www.ingramcontent.com/pod-product-compliance
Lightning Source LLC
LaVergne TN
LVHW070219080526
838202LV00067B/6855